TEN KEYS TO MORE

MANAGEMENT SUCCESS

By

David Randall

First Printing: 2016

ISBN 978-1-365-41540-1

Lulu Publishing

CHAPTERS

CHAPTER 1

DISCIPLINE MEANS CHAMPIONSHIP

Discipline, according to Webster's Dictionary, is "training that corrects, molds, or perfects the mental faculties or moral character." Many people try very hard to discipline themselves but are unable to do so. This is not necessarily a weakness, but it is definitely a weakness not to recognize you have that problem. Recognizing this weakness is the first step in remedying it.

It takes strength to admit you have a problem. I was once a smoker. It was causing me to have health problems, so I decided one day that when I finished the last cigarette in the package, I was not going to get any more.

Was this easy? Not by any means. One day, I was working on an old car and decided to take a break. I usually smoked a cigarette when I took a break, but I didn't have any. I wanted one so bad, I searched that old car for just a butt, but couldn't find one. I started to get in my car and go buy a pack. Then, discipline kicked in. I told myself that was not the thing I should do. I overcame that desire over a period of time and now I cannot tolerate being around someone smoking. When you make a commitment, you must stay with it.

Many people are disciplined in their quest for success in their profession, but are undisciplined in their personal lives, which ultimately causes them to suffer for it in all areas of their lives.

Being unable to discipline ourselves involves many facets of our lives. It is difficult to stay focused when there are personality conflicts with someone on the job. We sometimes feel hurt and cry out against the unfairness of life itself when we or our loved-ones have been treated unfairly are in pain through no fault of our own.

That is why personal growth as a lifetime commitment is so important. When we are making progress in our lives, it's easier to handle distractions by people who are not disciplined. Discipline itself frequently brings pain, but the pain is temporary, while the growth is permanent.

An athlete can never be a champion without some suffering. That can also apply to a business manager; you must have a plan to handle that suffering. The plan must be specific, well-thought-out, and perfected before the need arises.

In the worlds of athletics, business, or other fields, champions have to work through the pain particular to their field of endeavor. They start and keep going; they don't procrastinate and they don't quit.

I thought I knew what discipline was, until I went into the Air Force. During boot camp, I discovered what commitment and discipline were all about very quickly. When they said 6:00 am, they did not mean 6:01. I had to pay attention to every meticulous detail: the precision of the drill, the crease in the trousers and the shirt, the shine on the shoes, the way the beds were made, and how the living quarters were kept. My wife says she is glad I had this experience because she has never had to pick up after me.

The best way to develop pride and many other positive qualities is taught in personal responsibility in daily endeavors. In our society today, we do not see enough pride in personal appearance and performance on the job. It's also unfortunate how we clutter our schools, streets, highways, and other public places with trash.

In the military, pride is an important part of the training-pride in excelling in personal performance, getting a job done, and maintaining the honor and integrity of the service.

Another important quality the military teaches is obedience. When an individual's life is at stake, obedience is vital. That is why military personnel are taught through discipline that commands are to be obeyed, not questioned.

Being in the military taught me many positive qualities of success and helped me to organize myself and answer the call when combat is inevitable. It has made me become a more disciplined and understanding manager in business.

CHAPTER 2

DO YOU HAVE THE TIME?

We have all heard the phrase "Time is money," haven't we? Well, I believe that time has much greater value than money. It is the most precious and greatest commodity we have in our possession. It is renewed to an equal amount for everyone each day. We all have a renewable source, giving us each twenty-four hours daily.

Time is allocated to us in the small increments of seconds, minutes, and hours. Its value is determined by what we do with it. We cannot control the allocation of nor the passing of time. It is constantly moving beyond our grasp and we cannot borrow from the future. We must utilize it or it will be lost. As we go about our daily routine, we must utilize certain amounts of our allocated time for required daily activities such as eating, sleeping, and caring for our body. Approximately half of our time is consumed by these required tasks, thus the remainder necessitates frugal planning if we are to maximize the returns from our allocated daily time.

Most of us spend eight hours at our place of employment; these are the hours I wish to discuss. Only you can control how to utilize your time; no one can take it from you. It cannot be stolen unless you allow it to be. Have you ever said, "I didn't have time to..." or "If I only had more time I would have..."? Remember, we are all given exactly the same amount of time every day, and we must utilize our time or maximize our allotment to its best use. Our success depends upon it!

Within our daily routine—without regard to our duties as a clerk, computer operator, supervisor, production worker, salesman, etc.—there is always some off-time within that routine. These are "odd moments": gaps in our true function or a lull in our involvement. These "odd moments" are important and can be very constructive. What would we do without them? I challenge you to recognize these moments and to begin to utilize them to achieve a promotion within your workplace.

Did you know that with little or no additional time you could create a substantial increase in your income? This can be accomplished by stretching your imagination to find improvements for your employer/company and keeping your mind on planning, your schedule, your health, and a multitude of other things. Spend at least ten to fifteen minutes each day reading good materials relative to your occupation and seriously thinking about what you have read during your "odd moments". You will be surprised how much your attitude, job performance, and knowledge can be improved.

Every moment made useful is more profitable and helps you move toward living your life to its fullest potential.

I was visiting with a young man recently who had been with his present employer for only a few months. He told me how utilizing some of his odd moments paid off with each bonus. He is employed by a multi-million dollar international company, so he is not by any means within the ranking elite. This young man told me he delivered some materials to the laboratory for further testing and was informed that the test equipment was not functioning. He asked what the problem was and was told, "It just doesn't work." He was hesitant to say or do anything since he was a "new hire", but he needed the material tested to continue production. So, he told the machine operator's supervisor that he had about ten years of experience in operating and maintaining similar equipment and asked if he could take a look at the machine. In less than five minutes, the equipment was fixed and back in operation. The young man returned to his job area of production and said nothing to anyone with whom he worked. Two days later, he received a $25 bonus for what he had done. A letter was also placed in his personal file by his supervisor, stating that the company was extremely pleased with his cooperation and attitude, and for displaying such an excellent team-effort to work toward the goals of the company.

So, you see, sometimes we are rewarded immediately for our odd moments, and other times we earn the recognition later. We must remember that we are given time; how we use it is up to us.

CHAPTER 3

DREAMS AND GOALS

As a manager, I have learned that you can't have dreams or set goals for anyone but yourself. Goals must be personal and yours alone. As parents, we can help our children discover their talents and abilities, which will help them gain a better understanding of what they can do in life before they set their goals. However, parents cannot set their children's goals for them. God has a plan for each of our lives – a plan that includes personal growth and development as individuals.

Personal goals usually fit into corporate goals. As a manager, it is necessary to sit down with your group and discuss individual goals in order to see if they fit in with the company goals. Discuss how the group's goals reflect individual goals, and how they can work together for the good of the company. The key is that an individual's goal must be personal.

I once had a young woman, Gayla, working in production; she was very good at her job and had been with me for years. One day, she came to me and told me that her goal was to become the bookkeeper for the company. At that time, I had a very responsible bookkeeper and had no reason to replace her. A couple years later, my bookkeeper decided to leave to help her husband in his business. I could not stand in Gayla's way for the promotion, although I hated to lose her in production. She was not experienced in the position, but she assured me she could learn about it. She became the fastest and best bookkeeper I ever had. She knew what she wanted and went for it, but I, as her manager, could not set that goal for her; it was her personal goal.

We should always write our goals down on paper. When we see our goals written out, it reminds us to act. When we wish them in our mind alone, they are usually forgotten. Your goals must be thought-out, written down, and acted upon. Otherwise, they are meaningless.

Years ago, I decided to apply for a position I knew had become available. At the time, I was working as financial manager at a large organization and had been there about eight years. I interviewed for the position of assistant comptroller of a large corporation. During the interview, the comptroller asked me what my goals were for this position. I thought for a minute, looked at him, and said, "I want your job." He looked at me rather shocked, and then I continued to tell him that as he moved up, I wanted to move into his position. He hired me because that gave him a new goal. Within about one year, I had his job and he also had a better job. I'm not sure he ever thought about moving up until I came along.

Having dreams and setting goals must be an ongoing process; every time you achieve one goal, God gives you the ability and the grace to work toward another.

Our personal and professional goals must also be compatible with each other. You should never have a goal for your financial life that conflicts with your goals for your family life. The goals in all areas of your life must be compatible. However, a good manager should remind his people that they can change as their life situations change. That's why it's important to write down all of their goals, discuss them with family, and updated those goals as life situations change.

I've seen managers who have lost good leaders in the company because their professional and personal goals were not compatible – too much work and not enough family.

As managers, we must teach our employees to have goals and dreams and help them achieve those goals. By doing this, we can build a strong company and have happy employees at the same time. You must see what your "real self" could be and grow into that person. Successful people are willing to pay the price and do the things necessary in order to achieve their dreams and goals.

CHAPTER 4

HANGING TOGETHER

Back in the 1950s, I had spent eighteen months in Japan with the United States Air force during the Korean War, away from my wife and family. It was time to go home, and we were all excited to get there before Christmas.

As we began our long trip across the waters on a troop ship, everything was going along well until we came into a terrible storm. With forty-foot waves washing over the deck, almost everyone was so sick they wouldn't do any of their assigned duties.

The troop ship could not move for about three days. I was one of very few who did not get sick, so I was put on duty guarding the door going up on deck. No one was allowed on deck because they would be washed off by the waves. The men were sick and they just wanted to get some fresh air, but it was my responsibility to keep them below deck. For many, I had to use force by shoving, kicking, or whatever it took to keep them safe.

Many times I was tempted to let them pass and get some fresh air, but I had to follow orders and I knew these men needed to get home to their families, too. If I let them up on deck, they probably would have fallen overboard. I knew this storm was only temporary, and if we all would hang together in this rough time, we would all reach our goal of being home for Christmas Eve.

My point is this: during this stormy time, we were a group of men who suddenly became a society of equals. We had to all work together, and our ranks didn't matter. It was difficult to push an officer back down below when he had rank over me.

I learned a great deal from this experience, including to never demean yourself as the "little guy". Always take the responsibility given to you, which can be very useful later on. It's also strictly our attitude that allows us to learn.

I was very young when I had this great responsibility of helping to save lives, but for me, it was the opportunity for leadership that had tapped me on the shoulder and said, "It's you, buddy." However, there's a big difference between being ready and being prepared.

When the opportunity comes, you have to use every resource at hand, which I have tried to do over the years. As a manager, you have to take a stand to be trusting, firm, and fair. You must hang together, even when the going gets rough. A house divided cannot stand – we must all work together to accomplish the goal.

A leader exists to serve the employees and to create an environment in which their talents can flourish; that is the leader's obligation. The only way to do that is with communication, which doesn't just include using words. Actions must be used to show them you'll go the extra mile. However, you also have to know when to push and demand.

A leader must have the support and trust of his/her group. Trust is the lubrication that makes it possible for organizations to work. A leader knows right away who is with him and who is against him.

Being a manager or leader is a great responsibility and you must be willing and prepared for the job. It also takes time, experience, and patience. With trust, people begin to see patience for what it actually is – an intelligent choice an indispensable investment.

It takes time to build both trust and a covenant. The power of a covenant is known to every great business an organization in the world. It must be renewed regularly. So, if we "hang together" in good times and rough, we'll be successful as a team.

CHAPTER 5

OUTRAGEOUS MANAGEMENT

I was visiting with the president of a medium-sized corporation recently and he told me about an incident which took place at the company while he was on vacation. The chairman of the Board of Directors came to the corporate offices and was reviewing the financial records – nothing inherently wrong with that. However, during the review, he found that a large amount of money had been expended for shop maintenance.

Right away, he began to interrogate the bookkeeper about this "outrageous amount." Of course, the bookkeeper could only pull the invoices for him to review; she had nothing to do with the costs involved and didn't have any knowledge as to what the items on the invoices meant.

The Chairman created an ugly situation because he could not understand the reasons for the charges he saw. He told the bookkeeper that from that day forward, any maintenance costing more than $500 had to be specifically approved by him.

Of course, when the President returned from his vacation, the Chairman was already gone for the day. So, the bookkeeper informed him about what had happened; she was quite upset by the verbal tirade from the Chairman.

Within a few days of this incident, a key machine on one of the production lines went down. It required two items to fix it: a control switch costing $300 and an electric motor costing $545. The maintenance manager ordered the control switch, but when he started to order the motor, he was told he needed to talk to the President first. So, the President called the Chairman and confronted him with the situation. He told the Chairman that the production line was idle due to the breakdown and explained that he needed approval to place the order for the motor.

The Chairman was not pleased with the call and said, "I really did not mean what I said...go ahead and buy the motor, we need the production line running." How do you think the employees feel about their upper-level management after this episode?

We each have our areas of responsibility within the organization in which we are employed. At every level, from top to bottom, each person must be trusted to fulfill his/her respective job with integrity, loyalty, and responsibility. No one individual can make all the decisions or know everything that's going on within the organization.

Micro-managing creates havoc with scheduling, productivity, and interpersonal relationships, and destroys team incentives. Every manager must trust each member of his/her group. He must give to each person the responsibility for performing to his/her best ability. Along with responsibility, the authority of decision-making must also be given. Only then can a real team effort produce the desired results – all the members begin to understand that they control their own destiny and help each other to accomplish the goals set before them.

You see, what the Chairman doesn't understand is that he created a situation which changed the employees' attitudes; they went from being cooperative to a group of people who would work only as hard as they have to in order to get paid. As Carnegie said, "You can make your employee give you cooperation (until your back is turned) by threatening." You must show people that you trust, respect, and care about them in order to maintain a motivated team.

CHAPTER 6

PROPER TRAINING LEADS TO SUCCESSFUL TEAMS

Try to imagine your reaction if your manager were to call you into his/her office and make this request: "Please investigate and give me a brief report concerning..." Would you immediately say, "Of course, I'll get right on it."?

I think not. You would probably ask several questions, including one or more of the following: "What is that?" "Where do you want me to look?" "Is that part of my job?" "Why don't you have Mary do it?"

By the time your superior answers all of your questions, he could have accomplished the task himself. Even if all the questions were answered and explained as to how to find the information and why it is wanted, you would then probably get someone else to help or to go find the information for you.

Can you be entrusted to cheerfully and willingly take responsibility and do your share of the work for yourself and for the benefit of the organization, or is that "not your job"? As a member of any organization, it is important that each person work and function as a team.

Every member is a manager, just at different levels. Each must reach out to help others and, at the same time, perform at their maximum level of efficiency. In our society, there are many wanderers – people going from job to job – who often have harsh words about the management of prior employers. Unfortunately, these vagabonds receive a great deal of media attention due to being unemployed. However, our news media say nothing about the management teams that grow old and grey before their time due to their tireless, patient efforts to obtain quality, desirable persons willing to do their share as team members.

Too many times, the employee does nothing but loaf and criticizes when the manager turns his back, and refuses to accept the fact that he/she must give a day's labor for a day's pay. Go into any business, factory, or retail store, and you will most likely find a constant turn-over of workers, as the employer sends workers away who have shown lack of capacity to contribute to the interest of the business.

As a manager, it is your responsibility to take all employees assigned to your group and groom them to become a vital part of our team. Consequently, the responsibility for the ultimate development of those members rests on your shoulders. You must make them feel important to the group by creating in them a real sense of purpose and letting them know that they are working for a valuable and mutually important goal. Encourage them and teach them. Answer all their questions and believe in their abilities. This is of paramount importance to everyone within the team.

Dale Carnegie once said, "There is only one way under heaven to get anybody to do anything, and that is by making the other person want to do it. Remember, there is no other way." This desire has to be instilled from the top down.

I recently spent many hours in a major health care facility. During all of my time, spanning some two years, I never at any time saw any employee who did not have a smile on his/her face. They were constantly asking if they could be of assistance, whether to give directions or to escort me to my destination. I never heard a cross word spoken between them or to the clientele.

I commented about this to several people and was told this was not the case just a few years before. The new administrator (CEO) made the change by requiring all personnel to go through a training program where they learned that the only reason any organization exists is for the clientele. We are in the "people business" – personal relationships is all that really matters. Even a production worker on a manufacturing line serves as an ambassador to the client. Shoddy work results in bad merchandise, and in turn disgusts the consumers, driving them to other sources for the product.

So, as a manager, you must motivate your group, train them, counsel them, praise them, and help them achieve their goals through their team

efforts.

CHAPTER 7

PROTECTING OUR TERRITORY

People are somewhat like territorial animals. We all want to stake-out our territory. We want to strike back if we feel our turf is being threatened, whether in our business or family lives. We get caught up in constant power struggles.

Don't smother your competitive instincts, but harness them for the benefit of the company. Just how do good managers balance cooperation and competition? They must make that fighting instinct work for them instead of tearing the business apart.

I once had an employee who had been with the company for many years. She was good at her job, but never wanted anyone else learning about her job because she felt they would be "treading on her turf". It came time to put her heavy load into a computer. I finally convinced her it would make her job easier and would be more efficient. After learning how to use the computer, she realized it was better for both her and the company. However, she was not easy to convince.

Trying too hard to be clever in defending your turf can make for short-range thinking. Sometimes, the greatest "infighters" find ways to stab themselves with their own daggers more deeply than they ever cut an adversary.

Your hard work and good attitude will bring you everything you desire and you won't have to force it; it will simply catch up to you. However, not all people behave fairly. Good people do sometimes end up getting stepped on, either by management or their own co-workers. Although, by being honest and holding on to their beliefs, they'll eventually get aligned with the right management and co-workers.

In order to be a successful manager, you have to be a good leader. Your employees are your team; if you can get the whole team behind you, they will stick with you, even if it means stepping out of their territory. When my team is working with me instead of for me, it's a sign of their impression of me as a manager.

When I first purchased my business in the early 1970s, it was in financial trouble. I know I was taking on the big responsibility of turning it around, but I always liked a new challenge. I knew I had to have a good team behind me to accomplish this. I had to weed out a few "bad seeds" and add some good ones who wanted the company to be a success. Many had to cross over into other territories and work extra hours in order for it to be a successful business. I think I learned more about management in those three years than I ever dreamed I could. The experience made me a much stronger person and leader. It took us about three years to get the company

back on track, but we did it.

Give your employees a pat on the back, and

tell them that survival overrides territorial instinct

and that having a hand in success is more

important than being personally indispensable.

Their energy and enthusiasm will take on new

lives of their own.

As a manager, you cannot think of yourself

first. You have to believe that if you help everyone

around you to become successful, then the

success of the company will always follow. Then,

we will all reap the rewards as the team that wins

the game.

When we can step outside our territory and learn about more positions within the company, everyone will become successful, including the manager. The climb to success begins when your team comes together selflessly and can put aside all "turf wars" and selfish behaviors.

CHAPTER 8

THE IMPACT OF ATTITUDE

To me, attitude is more important than facts, education, money, circumstances, failures, and even success. It can make or break a company, or even your home.

The former owner of my company was a well-educated man, very knowledgeable of the business and seemed to be on the right track. I had been hired on as his accountant. After a few months, his father died and his attitudes toward the business completely changed. One day, he left and no one knew where to find him. The company was nearing bankruptcy.

Being the accountant, I had a choice to make: walk away, knowing all the employees would be without a job, or do something about it. I finally found him playing lead guitar in a night club. My wife and I decided to purchase the business if we could work it out with him. His attitude at that point was "let's do it". We made up a contract on a napkin and worked out the details later.

The remarkable thing is that we have a choice every day regarding the attitude we embraced from that day on. We cannot change our past or the fact that people act in a certain way. The only thing we can do is make use of one thing – attitude. We are in charge of our attitudes.

Positive thinking is sometimes misunderstood by many people. Some people honestly believe that positive thinking can enable you to do anything, while others believe it is no help at all. Positive thinking will let you use your abilities and experiences to their maximum potential. However, it must be realistic. I consider myself an optimistic, positive thinker, but if I needed major surgery, I would not have my accountant perform it. Unrealistic expectations are the seeds of depression.

Human beings do have certain limitations. There is a persistent belief that if you can conceive an idea and believe you can accomplish it, you will be able to do so. Your chances do increase dramatically if you really believe you can do it. However, many bankruptcies are filed by people who had this marvelous idea and believed with all their hearts they could achieve them. They poured their hearts, blood, sweat, and tears into their endeavors, and still ended in bankruptcy. Perhaps the idea was not sound or they didn't have the right skills, abilities, or training necessary to make the idea work. It could be that circumstances beyond their control prevented them from bringing their ideas to a successful conclusion.

We were given our minds so we can gather information, mix it with common sense, and ultimately make sound judgements about what we can and want to do. Then, we can plan accordingly. Common sense usually is not found in a book.

During those three years of struggling to bring my company back from near bankruptcy was very difficult. I had to make some major changes and it was a rough time for everyone, including my own family. However, I firmly believe that regardless of what was going on out there, my attitude gave me a competitive advantage.

In the years after getting back on track, we still had our ups and downs. I did have a number of good people behind me and those people did extremely well in their personal and business lives. What set the successful people apart? Attitude and momentum.

Action changes attitudes and performance. For example, our youngest son was very small during his high school years (about 5'6" and 130 lbs.), but he really wanted to play football. He knew he had to work hard in order to accomplish that, but he knew he could do it. He worked out, ate right, and built up muscle. He became the fastest and best running-back the team had. He had the right attitude to get the job done. Fortunately, your attitude is something you can control, and it starts with you.

CHAPTER 9

THINK LIKE A LEADER

We must remind ourselves that we are not pulled to high levels of success; rather, we are lifted there by those working beside and below us.

Achieving high-level success requires the support and the cooperation of others. It also requires leadership ability: getting others to do things you know they wouldn't do if they were not being led.

As leaders or managers, we sometimes have to trade minds with people in order to influence them. For example, when giving orders or handing out assignments, think to yourself,

"Would I like to carry out an order or assignment if it were given to me the way I give orders to other people?" Or when giving work instructions, think "Looking at this from the viewpoint of someone who is new to this, have I made myself clear?"

A telephone manner is also very important. Always say to yourself, "If I were the person on the other end of the line, what would I think of my telephone voice and manners?" One day, one of the women in purchasing called a supplier about shipping some material to my company. For some reason, he became very irate, calling her names and putting her down; it had her in tears. She finally had to hang up on him, and then came to me about the incident. I could not have him treating my employees in that manner, so I called him and cancelled all orders with him. I did not have to say anything else; he knew exactly why he lost my business.

About two months later, he drove from another state to my place of business and apologized for his actions on the phone. He was the sales manager of his business, and I don't think he would have appreciated that type of telephone conduct in his business.

We must think before we speak, but we must also think about our appearance. As leaders, we need to set the example. I sometimes helped in different areas of production when there was a problem, so I dressed in jeans and tee shirts. I noticed my employees started treating me like their co-worker, with no respect. I decided it was time for an appearance change. I started wearing a suit, with a white shirt and tie. It was an amazing difference. I was respected as the manager. My supervisor personnel began to change their appearances as well, and they also began to get more respect.

As leaders, we must use different approaches to leadership situations. We could assume the position of a dictator who makes all decisions without consulting those affected. He refuses to hear his subordinates' side of an issue because, deep down, he might be afraid the subordinates might be right and this would cause him to lose face. I have worked with a few people like this. Dictators usually do not last long. Employees may fake loyalty for a while, but unrest soon develops. Some of the best employees leave, and those remaining get together and plot against the tyrant. The result is that the organization ceases to function smoothly. This puts a bad light on the dictator with his superior.

And then we have those leaders who go strictly "by the book." However, problems arise that you cannot always find in a book. I once had a technician who was very knowledgeable. He came to me one day with a problem with a machine that he couldn't solve. I went back, studied the situation, and gave him my opinion on the matter. However, it wasn't "in the book", therefore he believed it couldn't work that way. I asked him to give it a try because it was not working his way. Reluctantly, he did it my way and it worked. I had to teach him that sometimes you just have to use "common sense". I also had to let him know that I respected what he was doing and that I was there to help him in every way I could.

You may be the manager, but you must have that team beside you and below you to be successful. Many times, I thought to myself, "What kind of company would this be if everyone in it were just like me?"

CHAPTER 10

WHO'S RESPONSIBLE?

Taking responsibility for your behaviors and your actions instead of believing that society must forgive you because it's "not my fault" is the quality most needed today.

Do you honestly believe there is something you can do to make your life better or worse? I think so. I don't care how hard (or good) my life may be – I can change it, and the choice is mine. The responsibility for yourself is the day you stop making excuses and start working on your way to the top.

If you sincerely do accept responsibility for your own future, you are within a step of some serious progress in your life. This can be earth-shattering because, until you accept responsibility for your future, it is left to chance, which can be cruel. The good news is that you were off to a great start even before you were old enough to make choices. You were planned long ago. Your mother and father may not have specifically planned you and they may not have thought the timing of your arrival was perfect, but I assure you that you are the winner you were meant to be.

Our youngest daughter had two children: a girl and a boy. Both were cute little redheads. That was her perfect family, and that was it for her. Well, nature took its course and she found out she was expecting another child; she just couldn't believe it. But after her daughter arrived, she became the joy of the whole family. My daughter never called her a mistake, but always said she was her "bonus baby."

Now it is time for you to have a game plan. You should plan, prepare, and expect your level of success. If you are not happy with your current level of success, you must change your plans and preparations, as well as your expectations for the future.

We can all make a difference in our world. Unfortunately, too many of us throw our hands up and say. "What can I do? I am only one person."

Well, you can reach down and extend a helping hand to people in need or speak a word of encouragement to those around you and through them, influence countless other people. The life you live makes quite a statement.

I have a friend who says, "But Dave, you just don't understand about my past." I have counseled with him many times; he has come a long way, but has a long way to go still. I tell him it's not what has happened to you that make a difference in your life, but how you handle what has happened; it's where you finish that counts.

We must all use what we have; many people do not put their talents to good use. We are stewards of our talents and it is our responsibility to develop and use them. Many people find it comfortable to deny a talent. They use the excuse "Poor little me, I don't have an education," or "I have a handicap. I don't have what it takes to be successful."

A few years ago, I was attending a convention and met a man who was very friendly and outgoing. I noticed he had a slight problem – he honestly could not walk and talk at the same time. As we walked along, he always had to stop when he began to speak. I asked him what type of work he did; he appeared to be a successful man. He said he was in a business that was always picking up. He owned his own garbage business in a large city and had become a very wealthy man.

He had a vision and, even in his line of work, it required persistence, the right attitude, and responsibility to make it a reality, but he was enjoying the benefits of his persistence. To do the things we really want to do require a considerable amount of effort. It's tough sometimes, but the rewards are great.

-The End-

www.ingramcontent.com/pod-product-compliance
Lightning Source LLC
Chambersburg PA
CBHW022134170526
45157CB00004B/1876